Sermonette

What Type of Christian Are You? Pick a Letter or Letters (A–Z)!

Susie Sanders

Special Program

ISBN 979-8-89043-856-0 (paperback)
ISBN 979-8-89043-857-7 (digital)

Christian Faith Publishing
832 Park Avenue
Meadville, PA 16335
www.christianfaithpublishing.com

Printed in the United States of America

Greetings to All!

Prayer

Let us pray. Father God, thank you for giving us another chance to see a brand-new day. Father God, we give you all the honor and praise. Father God, you see where I am. I am not even sure how I got here. I know that it was on your calendar—this day, at this time, and at this place—for me to be here. I see no way out, so I ask that you send down your holy spirit in this place. I ask that you bring the wisdom and encouragement that comes only from you. Help me think big because I do not limit you. Help me be sensitive to your voice and trust you beyond my fears and doubts. Father God, you are the God of fire by night and the cloud by day as we go through our wilderness experiences.

Father God of Joshua, bring down the walls of impossibilities. Father God of Daniel, close the mouths of those who seek to destroy and hinder us. Father God, speak peace to the storms that rage in our lives. Father God, give us the strength to continue to look to the hills from which cometh all our help. Father God, touch, heal, and deliver us; set us free; and continue to watch over our families, loved ones, and friends. Father God, keep us covered under the blood of Jesus. In the mighty name of Jesus the Christ, I pray for all. Amen!

What Type of Christian Are You? Pick a Letter or Letters (A–Z)

1. *A Christian.* This is a person who is always ready to work for the Lord, always willing and always doing. This person appreciates what others are doing. This person is achieving a potential goal through God's Word. This is a person who shows action by walking the walk and not talking the talk. This person wears a coat of armor, giving and not asking. The word says, "Whatever I ask in Jesus' name shall be given unto me: For we walk by Faith, not by sight" (2 Corinthians 5:7). Amen!

2. *B Christian.* A B Christian says that they can't do it because they have a headache; they have a stomachache; it's raining; they have pain in their legs; they work too late; they have nothing to wear; they didn't get their nails, toes, and hair done; they don't like the preacher; they stay too long; the choir can't sing; the church always asks for money… The list goes on and on. When I hear this, I open my Bible to Matthew 5:3–10: "Blessed are the poor in spirit for theirs is the kingdom of heaven. Blessed are they that mourn for they shall be comforted. Blessed are the meek for they shall inherit the earth. Blessed are they which do hunger & thirst after righteousness for they shall be filled. Blessed are the merciful for they shall obtain mercy. Blessed are the pure in heart for they shall see God. Blessed are the peacemaker for they shall

be called the children of God. Blessed are they which are persecuted for the righteousness sake for theirs is the kingdom of heaven." B Christians, Believe, Be Kind and Be Thankful.

3. *C Christian.* A C Christian is one who is committed to the Lord. This person is Christlike. This person can adjust to any changes and make connections with all. This is a caring and sharing person. "Come to me, all you who labor, are heavy laden, I will give you rest. Take my yoke upon you & learn from me, for I am gentle and lowly in heart, and you will find rest for you souls and for my yoke is easy and my burden is light" (Matthew 11:28–30).
4. *D Christian.* A D Christian is a person who decided to follow Jesus and not the crowd or the peer pressure of the world. "Do not say, 'I will repay evil'; Wait

for the Lord and he will rescue you" (Proverbs 20:22).

5. *E Christian.* An E Christian is a person who shares encouragement with others. This is someone who has lot of energy and exercises their mind, body, and soul for eternal life. "Therefore, encourage one another and edify one another" (1 Thessalonians 5:11).
6. *F Christian.* An F Christian is a fake Christian—a person who believes in false prophets; a person who worships their house, clothes, cars, money, rabbit foot, idol gods, and other things; a person who has many doubts and fears; and a person with weak or no faith. "For as the body without spirit is dead, so faith without work is dead" (James 2:26).
7. *G Christian.* A G Christian is a great person and a Godly person who has seven keys: strong faith, peace, hope, joy, hap-

piness, prosperity, and love. "Greater is he that's living in me than he that is in the world" (1 John 4:4). God of Abraham, Isaac, Jacob, your family, friends, loved ones, you, and me. Glory!

8. *H Christian.* An H Christian is a person who is hopeful, humble, honest, and helpful and has a heavenly spirit. The Bible teaches us that "faith is the substance of things hoped for, the evidence of things not seen" (Hebrews 11:1).
9. *I Christian.* An I Christian is a person who is intelligent, imaginable, and involved with Jesus and shares inspirational thoughts. I am so glad that trouble don't last always. "I have called you friends" (John 15:15).
10. *J Christian.* A J Christian is a person who is joyful and knows Jesus is alive. Jesus said, "I am the way, the truth and the life. No one comes to the father except

through me" (John 14:6). "Weeping may endure for a night, but Joy comes in the morning" (Psalm 30:5).

11. *K Christian.* A K Christian is a person who knows who you are, what they want, what God wants you to know, what is best for you, when you need it, and how much you need, so keep your promises and know Jesus as your King. "God, the Lord, is my strength" (Habakkuk 3:19).
12. *L Christian.* An L Christian is a person who is lovable and knows Jesus is Lord. The Lord loves you with an everlasting love. He has a plan, a position, and a purpose for your life. Jesus is the Light of the world. "I am the resurrection and the life" (John 11:25).
13. *M Christian.* An M Christian is a person who is merciful and a miracle worker. This is a person who gives donations willingly, feeds the hungry, gives a drink

to the thirsty, clothes the naked, shelters the homeless, comforts the imprisoned, visits and cares for the sick shut-ins, and buries the dead. "My soul wait only upon God and silently submit to him for my hope and expectation are from him" (Psalm 62:56). Pause! Question: Are the letters *A* to *M* soaking in yet? Say twice. Continue.

14. *N Christian.* An N Christian is a person who feels like they are nothing and go through depression (e.g., "I am just a nobody!). Well, today I know somebody who can save anybody, and his name is Jesus. He is the Prince of Peace, the Mighty God, the Lamb of God, Mary's baby, God's son, the Son of Man, Wonderful, a Counsellor, the Alpha and Omega, the Everlasting Father, the Good Shepherd, our Savior, the Lily of the Valley, the Bright Morning Star, the

Great I Am, the Lord of Lords, the King of Kings, the Healer, the Light of the World, and many more titles. Today is a new year, a new morning, a new day, or a new beginning. It's time for a new plan, new feelings, and new opportunities, so never give in or give up. "He said to her, 'Daughter, your faith has made you well, so go in peace'" (Luke 8:48).

15. *O Christian.* An O Christian is a person who is on-going, on-knowing, and on-doing. This is a person who opens doors for others. "Only fear the Lord and serve him faithfully with all your heart, for consider how great the things, he has done for you" (1 Samuel 12:24).
16. *P Christian.* A P Christian is a person who is a prayer warrior and keeps the peace. In the Bible, 2 Corinthians 3:17 says, "Now the Lord is the Spirit, and where the Spirit of the Lord is there is

liberty." Praise the Lord! Precious Lord, take my hand.

17. *Q Christian.* A Q Christian is a person who is quiet. "Hush! Listen! Somebody is calling your name" was said by a church member at church. "There is a sweet spirit in this place, and it is the spirit of the Lord. 'Hear counsel, receive instruction & accept corrections that you may be wise in time to come' [Proverbs 19:20]" was said by another church member at church. These are two of my great mentors, sorority sisters who are heavenly bound. They will never be forgotten and are always in my heart.
18. *R Christian.* An R Christian is a person who very religious. This is a person who knows the Word inside and out. The person is always willing to learn and makes sacrifices by doing, learning more, studying, and being trained by

others. "If you are willing and obedient, you shall eat the good of the land" (Isaiah 1:19). Repent, restore, rejoice, and relax!

19. *S Christian.* An S Christian is a person who is very spiritual and safe with the Holy Spirit, seeks knowledge, and wears the shoes of a servant. The question asked is "How are you today?" and the reply is "I am too blessed to be stressed. I am holding on daily, and I am pressing my way through." The Lord is my shepherd. The Lord is my strength and my shield. I seek and stand on the Lord's promises. "He who is greatest among you shall be your servant" (Matthew 23:11).
20. *T Christian.* A T Christian is a person who is thankful. Rev. Dr. Martin Luther King Jr. quoted that the time is always right to do what is right. There is no storm that God won't carry you through, no bridge that God won't help you cross,

and no battle that God won't help you win. Trust God, never give in, and never give up. Just look up and join Team Jesus. "Trust in the Lord with all your heart and he will show you the way" (Proverbs 3:5–6).

21. *U Christian.* A U Christian is a person who is unique and understanding and supports unity. "Let the same mind be in you that was in Christ Jesus" (Philippians 2:5).
22. *V Christian.* A V Christian is a person who is has the *victory*! Victory is mine. "Let everything that has breathes praise the Lord" (Psalm 150:6).
23. *W Christian.* A W Christian is a person who is a worker of God. This is a Christian who knows the Bible and a person who works hard and worships God. "Greater is he that is living in me than he that is in the world" (1 John 4:4).

24. *X Christian.* An X Christian is a person who has X-ray vision. We cannot see God, but we know he is here. "In the beginning, God created the heavens and the earth" (Genesis 1:1).
25. *Y Christian.* A Y Christian is a person who is young at heart. You are special. Be Yourself, spend time with Jesus, and pray. God is on your side (Romans 8:31).
26. *Z Christian.* A Z Christian is a person who is zealous. This is a person who zips their lips and listens. This person has two ears to listen more and one mouth so he may speak less. "For God so loved the world that he gave his only son that whoever believes in him should not perish, but have eternal life" (John 3:16).

In closing, I would like to share some personal testimonies. I lost my earthly father when he was at the age of seventy-seven. He was a WWII veteran. I lost my oldest brother, a great mentor to me. He was a high school educator, counselor, and minister in New York City. My mother was hit by truck while walking to work at the age of eighty-seven. She has had COVID-19 three times and pneumonia. She is still alive at ninety-three years young, and she will be ninety-four years young next month. (Glory!)

As for me am I perfect? No! I make many mistakes. I have been abused, used, broken, scorned, held at gunpoint, and robbed three times in my home. In the year 2020, I was diagnosed with a brain lesion, went to four different hospitals, became totally paralyzed from head to toe, and lost sight in my left eye, but God gave me amazing grace and mercy. And I am still in recovery. God said, "Susie?"

I said, "Yes, God?"

He said, "This *not* the end of your story." (Hallelujah!)

In closing, Adam was talking to God. Adam asked God, "Why did you make Eve so pretty?"

God said, "Adam, that is easy. It's so you will love her."

Adam said to God, "Why did you make her body so beautiful?"

God said to Adam, "That is easy. It's so you will love her."

Adam said to God, "I got one last question. Now, you know that Eve bit the forbidden fruit first, so why did you make her so dumb?"

God said to Adam, "That is easy. It's so she will love you."

Thank you for listening. I love you, and God bless you. Please think about the message and answer within your heart. I hope and pray that you enjoyed my story and were able to get something positive from it. I am Susie Sanders, and I'm *out*!

Ms. Susie Ann Walton Sanders: Autobiography

Favorite scripture: "Let not your heart be troubled: Ye believe in God, believe also in me" (John 14:1).

A servant of the church and in the community: Life member of Campbell Chapel African Methodist Episcopal Church

Past and present services: Sunday School Teacher; Church Treasurer; Financial Secretary; Steward Board; Trustee

Board; YPD Director; Assistant YPD Director; Brantley and Childers Women Missionary Society President; Pastor's Aide President; Choir Member; Vivian Bryant Angel Choir Director; WYDYK Board; Senior Usher Board; Vacation Bible School Teacher; Lay Member; Christian Education Department; Beautification Committee President; Rho Sigma Omega Chapter of Alpha Kappa Alpha Sorority, Inc.; Sheriff's Association; Library Board Trustee; School Tutor; Youth Mentor; Public Speaker; Honor Society; SABU Organization; Student Supportive Service; NAACP; Americus Area Gospel Music and Cultural Arts Workshop, Inc.; American Book Club; and Arts and Crafts Summer Program

Education: Bachelor of Science Degree from Georgia Southwestern State University; Master's Degree in Education from

Troy State University in Troy, Alabama; Specialist Degree in Education and Leadership from Troy State University; currently a Retired Educator

Employment: Second-, fourth-, and fifth-grade teacher in Dooly County Elementary School and paraprofessional in Cherokee Elementary School.

Committees past and present: Lead Teacher; Report Card Committee; Student Support Team; Parent Involvement Committee; Reading, ELA, Social Studies, and Science SAC committees; STEM Committee; and Black History Program Chairman.

Family: Susie is the daughter of the late Veteran Costell Walton Sr. and Mrs. Ozie Mae Hamilton Walton. She has one daughter (Mrs. Tamika La'Shon Walton Walker), one son-in-law (Mr. Courtland Fa'Shaun Walker Sr.), one grandson (Master Courtland Fa'Shaun

Walker Jr.), one granddaughter (Miss Courtney Ta'Mia Walker), four sisters, and six brothers, one of which is deceased.

Poem:

A Godly Woman

A woman of beauty,
a woman of grace, a
woman of excellence and
beholding God's face, she
walks with the Lord with
integrity, knowing her
purpose and destiny. No
matter what happens, she
walks in God's love and
reflects the beauty of her
heavenly Father above.

www.ingramcontent.com/pod-product-compliance
Lightning Source LLC
Chambersburg PA
CBHW022043150726
47990CB00004B/1598

9798890438560